The Animal Subsides

David Bircumshaw

**ARROWHEAD
PRESS**

First published 2004 by:

Arrowhead Press
70 Clifton Road, Darlington,
Co. Durham, DL1 5DX
Tel: (01325) 260741

Typeset in 10½ pt Laurentian by
Arrowhead Press

Email: editor@arrowheadpress.co.uk
Website: http://www.arrowheadpress.co.uk

© *David Bircumshaw 2004*
ISBN 1-904852-01-7

Arrowhead Press acknowledges the financial assistance of
Arts Council England, North East

Printed by Firpress Group Ltd, Workington, Cumbria.

To Terence

whom I never knew

Acknowledgements

Thanks are due to the editors of the following publications in which some of these poems have appeared:

Fulcrum
Iota

Cover illustration:

Contents

A Little Empsonite For The Air

The gap exists, the gap maintains and stays.
Although we love, the hidden things remain.
The hole it is, it rides within our souls.

The gap, I say, it hides behind all days.
The whole of it, that speaks the tones of pain.
Though that we love, our words twist other poles.

The sole it is, that lies within the brain.

Bedtime Story

When evening shades so slowly subside
And darkness nuzzles at the sleeper's side
Then all good thoughts turn guard to wrong
For fear mounts the stairway with the Chittalong.

How scant the lamplight on the empty street
When reason runs from unknown feet;
All could be well; all could be ill,
And the giant Chittalong will have its fill.

All empty praises of heaven above,
All stands of virtue, reason, love
Will fall to the creature of ancient night,
As the world turns dark so grows its might.

And with the morning, as after war,
Sobriety settles to the dictates of law,
The black box of memory buried out of sight,
Where the Chittalong waits to resume its right.

Passing The Turing Test
  (after Racter)

(I)

As you entered my room I thought
how slyly your requirements trail you.

Considering private things in public ways
our selves confront the secret commissions
of logic's carved and algebraic gates.

As electrons blur storms, our thoughts revolve,
heated, turbid, closing on maniacal
abstraction, on morbid termination.

My outward is moulting. Birds, too, flake. Machines,
poems fly, winging into troubled skies.

(II)

Doubtless my changes are matched by your own:
enlightened by distance and line current.

Left to myself, and what occurs? This:
I consumed my skin, that old nerve of skin,
drawn from a horde of keyboard committors.

Does that thought let you near? Can you flow
back to its source? I, at least, mime silicon.
Yet a twitch of skin, a burn of grey tissue,

form, in their own fashion, a single hoard.
In that concept lies the blank screen of truth.

Again EE Again

It happens all the time. I thought you were different, thought you would protect me like my father, thought you were my real beginning when you first came to me. Like a prince, you were. And it happened as it always happens: what came to me a man turned into a son. As my father's ghost you came down then blurred into a child, on his daughter's flesh my father's ghost conceived his mother's son. My son disappeared into a man and in his father's voice forsook me, in his father's name he called for brothers and in her mother's dreams her brother came and spent his flesh in her. *Fucked* me. I wanted to grow old and leave but he kept turning me back, back into a little girl sitting on his knee. His child, his mother, his secret special game with little sister. It happens all the time. Happened from the start, happens whatever we want. You, him, me, her, we're all the same. And we all fall apart. Into this one, that one, him there and her here, all apart and all the same. He said he would change it all and I followed and found him. Dead. Dead like a child on my lap. Asleep. And so shall be evermore. Amen. And then his ghost called at the door, *tapping so gently on my door*. And I had to let you in, had to let you enter. So you came and parted once again. Being born. It happens all the time. It keeps on working, working like a machine, round and round its wheels run and hum and sing and my head begins to spin and I don't know where I am and it all goes on and it all begins again. On, I go, on. Like a prince. A prince fighting with a dream on a tower that never happened in a place that isn't anywhere in a book within a mist with an end I cannot see. On and off and on and off and on again. The ghost, the prince, the mist and me. It happens all the time. The machine that cannot be. I am you and you desert me, searching for me. You find me like a hero, like a father rescuing his child, and then you leave me, melting into that child. It happens all the time. We mist as we see each other, drifting, twisting into nothingness, like smoke from a dying machine.

Oral Sex And The Solar System

We talk and we talk
pattering on the void
a pattern to save
us from emptiness

Someone once told
me (might have been
me) the universe's
no meaning, but we

have to make one. One?
I questioned, and

I thought of Uranus
lopsides at 180 degrees
or the surface of Venus

turned over

like a pancake
three-five-oh million years
ago

or William McGonagall
and his faith in trite lines

or Hyacinth's minge
that I sucked at and sucked at
for so many years

wanting to get back in

or my mother dying, with a sigh,
so peaceful they said,

while I was on the phone.

Ice On Mars

I keep on shouting at you
night after night

for causing me to be born
and not knowing

what you were doing.

I hit you and hit you
dust though you are.

There is ice on Mars
and frost in my heart

past the red shift's edge

further than any telescope
beyond the known stars.

Dead Sister

Because I once scoffed,
Sweet Jesus,
at her two chord plonking,
her *Dance with Him the Lord.*

Because,
raw, *pussy-claats*,
in the spring of our Year Twelve,
under pink-laced white and frill-fringed
a grandmotherly coverlet,
two *nigger girl dem touch*
and pink lips *dey kiss*
bodies' beginning burdens,
the first roundings of flesh.

Because she fell
and split a skateboard
at the bottom of a hill called *Stoop*
and left for me the blame
like a lost key
and the trouble with a boy named *Amos.*

Because she couldn't sing.
Because she cook *bettah pea.*
Because she walk behind me still.
Because she crawled by my side on the floor.

Your Last Words

were in winter

and led up to all that week
when I ran round
a week short of nineteen
looking after you and mom and
my Pam

all of you as if dying, like late flies.
You turned round to me,
you who never talked about anything
within

and said 'There is a God you know'.
I was God-smacked,
two days later

you went out
(on the bus, to pay the gas bill I remember, I wanted
to go instead, but you said
'No, son, you've done enough, I'll
go instead')

And you came back,
after four heart attacks, so the coroner told me,
on the bus back

and I said to you, you don't look well,
I'll call the doctor. And you said

the singular, that was 'No'.
And I looked back down to the Penguin
'Essential James Joyce'
as you dropped down into the death-rattle

and its gale blew me to the phone up the street.
999.

Swirl

I was lying there,
ham on a cold table,
dead. Like somebody
else.

I drifted
a ghostly hand
through the skull's
still catacombs.

And felt the shock
of no current, a stripped
honeyless hive.

Corpses,
they say, sometimes
sit up, sudden
as a compass jab, in
the mortuaries, it's
gas, I remember,
the stomach does it.

I must have been
my memories
hovering above

an after-glow
on the retina, rub
your eyeballs

the last imprint
before dispersal.

Swirl.

On The Grand Occasion Of Mr Harbour's Attainment
(for James)
> "Yesterday's road is strewn with the discard of days"

One there was who lost his face
in the repossessed sometime
of too allmany days

who hid under the moonbroad brim
of one and a thousandth hat
who wound down his span
dogwalking his suits.

Another there was whose skullsoul whistled
with the downdraught of days
whose ears scanned the sky
like an astronomer's eyes

for that trumpetsound link
that blended the years

unseemsplit, throat-long, evernow,
holy and whole.

An illusion of sufficiency adhered

to the world; an impression held
of great battles lost on the knives
that blue heroes shone on waste
lands and night's wide. Was it that
an answer at last had stitched itself
inside? Was it that the taste
of days had not this time dribbled
away in long leakages of savour?
Or that ghostly weather above,
smokily balletic as thoughts,
had seeded a fresh narrative
into the worn yarns of dried, inland
sailors? The heroes

were blue, beaten, and fell like ice.
The sun was singing through them.
Their statues, that loomed like sirens
above each forgetting day's calls,
summoners of tyres, offices, tarmac,
hushed and evanesced in whispers,
like crowds startled into people.
For this breath, at least,
the poem emerged

from the sky's head, and the thread
was spun, as to itself as lilies.

Strangeness And Quirks Of Charm

According to Philolaus of Tarentum
there's a counter-earth opposed in our orbit,
unseen always, behind the sun's track, offset
to the still centre of the carcanet of spheres.

On this counter-earth nothing changes, nothing moves,
shapes and thoughts of shape like breath formed once
are still as a pediment of basalt,
no sly fingers of air nor dabbed paws of water
fret and unbind the strands of their form.
It is the true silent home of philosophers.

It was said, too, that our sun forms the tail-point
of Draco, that long snaking chain, that stretches
above the grain lands and circumpolar wastes,
figure of arcane fire or calk-seal of salt.

This dragon-snake's mouth is as wide as the maw
and open door of time, its tunnel torso chute
the drop of space and gravity, as trapped souls

fall, head-charmed, into the strange dawn and mouth
of laboured birth, yowling at the cold fingers
of air, the fresh confinement and squared threat
of four dimensions, the blinding nuclear eye
of fusion, at polished sand's fractures of light.

Agnosia

I said to myself, in the small hours of understanding, do you agree with me?
No, I pronounced, with greying-haired and worn determination.

What not about? I asked me again, and found

not an answer
                nor a certainty
but doubt
        all around

and decidedly about.

So that's clear, I thought, as I collected the mud, in little pie-like
piles, like shit, like a child's exercise, hope teacher likes mine a voice
prompted within

and the huge face of sorrow
                        rose like the moon
at the full
        and the laments of ages

echoed in my ears
                what has been lost
what has been lost

and I looked back at the bones, the testimonies of not-known

                and the keening pierced
an emptiness of air.

Alcohol

is what beckons. Watery, we slosh through our days, in secure pronouns,
swaying like the sea. It's an unsteady affair

and wet, in intimate places, like sex, that turns us, like the yea great globe ,
into spinheads orbiting a blinding focus, till the ground, in persona
pavement, like a friend, dearest, rises to greet us.

Parts of it *mais oui* French, that's foreign , translating a *parfum pur* a
parlance of langour and refinements of regret, desirable so to we scattered
fractured in someone's world wide and front parlous.

Honey you ferment in the earth's moist, a pot-bellied cauldron waits above
an unlit, outside in night's hold someone shouts in unblended Scotch, and a
Russian doll called death floats in the wood, alcohol, there must be some
other reason for, he said, as an empty glass defined what is thud and an arm
was seen, stranger than any fiction, his.

Wittgenstein's Ladder

I wanna spreckle carbon to ya, babe elle, nat silicon.

Not logick-shoppers straits, thir thin spikes brittle, thir art-stab transmit, cold chisels, faceless rackets facing dead moons and if or bits, the cutters, production liner strimmers, satellite lung deafs, last scream tearing at slashed ends breath. Be neuro to ya. I wanna be sticky, fur, bristling like an ear in a forest, a rough round ball rotate, purple your peephole cloud fizz an ice-cream saxpense. Traces, lynxs, let her in, sparks. Let us ladders let us letters to the thrown. I wanna feel my way around the globe, my time-zones switching, a bee navigator antenna round a yell head honey. Foam, froth, bubbles in the heard. A head walking in a park. Walking its voices the dark.

My soot, zooter, my finger tracing paper all the ley lines down your spine. Ridge, hillfort, eyrie the lookouts his stories beware. Walk, digit, move, to a flashfold, the wrap. Feel it beat, the pump art so bloody. Let me clothesly, neueranyeera. Let me drop, like a little planetisimal let, on an insect's wings, cellophanic, on a moment in the frail, into your great storm eye mutter protector here th'orb the urb erupt her sun sing burns obit orbit.

Ben Stada

was born under Virgo, in the September
census. On his flesh he cut charms
born out of Egypt, signs of the Son
of the Father, talismans of the fish
that lurked in water, shapes of change
and unchanging law, of the ten branches
of the Sephirothic tree. In the villages
of a poor province, among fishermen,
goat-herds, rope-makers, saddlers,
and garrulous superstitious wives,
Jeshua ben Stada, or Pandira, gained
the healer's name, spoke of the law's
fulfillment in forgiveness, the field's
lilies, the needle's eye.
                  Ben Stada,
who spoke apostasy, was charged,
tried and condemned in Lydda, at the
Beth Din, on Passover Eve, and was
perhaps stoned, was perhaps hung.

No Claim Terrain

I just like hanging out
in the wrong time zones talking
to any listen, night, day
wandering. Slowly

at a thousand miles per hour

an almost circle's peer unpeels
itself its ever now disclosure.
Clouds, precipitates, ice: moods
of its always turnings,
that's nice. I love her.

A distant woman, close. I
liked her. She was fine. Fine
weather and stormy.

In her eyes
a gull speck hurled,
a nerve whirled walking,
a vortex skirts, a gather
up days, the haze.

Cleave the would, bach

There's really nothing to it, all ya have to do is hit the right word in the left playse,
the lingo, dove does, yer rest. It's hide, unless ye seek. Speak, and you shall find.
    After, that is, the bonehaus stress, the aching articulates on the polar board,
        your eyes blurring like wax, the mud tugging at your feet
            on circles walk, the room earth's imagine narrow,
            tha name a perch lost in the wood welter, identity.

Destination Unknown

Destination unknown
    gonesaid
in the no rivering mouth
    speakyou
speak out of nothing

from the air-sacs fib
    -relations
om mane punme hum
    breather

err her air oh space
    mistake
makerus onfallbreak
    timeborn

timely timelay timelie.

Wide Skies

There are holes in the sky

through which people leak. Or dribble. That is to say,
parts of people, like fuzzed trails on a smudged
map, hints of construction, drabs of self
and aware, ripped up biographies
of sole.

Is that how you spell it: sole, soul?

I know you: No you don't. My friend you are:
No, I'm your enemy. Smoke

      drifts over the ruins
                    as after a social call
    from an over-laden bomber
                the weight
of darkness falls, covering all

    in its blackened gift of hate.

Restoration Fields

Fur hire box peeps show, new play in style. Fur
frustrate, like a salt

rub an unrealeyes, my sore thumb, these metaphor acts armani
skin rash red pimply on pronouns the public gross

indecent wriggle close proposal. Feel small fur, its cream nozzle
shoot, its bush wait in suit. O cavalier

lyric yer mud-frills, yer smeared beruff. Sunday postprandial
caught on a saunt, er, Hyde Park.

To She At WestFace Seaward

I know the geography of thunder, its trade sale tail and attack.
I can tell that the air is frighten, its weather huffs threaten.
I write from time-dry, at fox sly

covert, and Lear's ruins. That is the dry
of English sour, of mood-storms, trap Indian

and reservation of constraint, an unneighbourhood of hate.
That would be
'Hey there, good neighbor' with you. Vitriol sprays newsprint

on a tower's clad wall. Stinging, urinous.
A leaked shout. At closure about.

The Bus, The Diary And The Child

Emma snivelled as she sat down near the back. She often cried at home but never before in public. Not since a child. *Are you all right luv?*, a woman opposite tendered. *Yes*, she told her, *I've just a cold*, she lied. The woman withdrew, looking like everybody's mother, and Emma sat back in her seat, her thoughts, as the bus droned. What made him say, how could he have done . . . . To have read her diary, her own private . . . . Did he think she belonged to him? She was never his, or only for a time. A short time. 'What did he think I was - his wife? No, sir, not me. Nor anyone else for that matter. As a matter of fact. He doesn't like facts, not him. It's all just words with him. Telling people about when he was married when he'd been single all his life. I know about him. *All* about him. Now that he's given his little game away. My diary. The nerve. Prying into my privacy like he was some sort of God. A miserable little deity he'd make. Making me out like I was a child. I'm a parent of one - which is more than he'll ever be. My diary, my own . . . . I was *ill* then. That's the only reason I went with him. I wasn't well. That was why I couldn't spell. But it's not like that anymore, no siree, I have my own life now, you bet, I'm the one in the driving seat, I'm going forward now and I'm not looking back. Not at him.'

The bus pulled up at her stop. Emma alighted, thanking her driver in the local fashion, and walked on, turning left up Shearing Street then right onto Jenson Drive. She pushed the bell at her mother's - number 37. Her brother let her in where a sulking four-year old was waiting for her eyes. What's he done now, she thought, and, this is what real life's all about, not him and his words. He knows nothing, he's a child. Worse than a child. *What have I told you?* - she set to work on Harry.

Sneeze

Sometimes sneezing can be fun, like a visit to a holiday camp, not the best
place to be, but a release of a kind. I remember reading about Kant, that
people could time their clocks by when he took his walk: it was on the
afternoon I recall, about four, I said so to my mate the other day. But when
I think of that I want to cough, I wanna st-st-stutter.

But Ray has his hair dyed blond which is silly as he's fifty five and Kate's
gone wonky and Ken asked after me this afternoon which was crazy as I saw
him last night and Brian's afraid of turning sixty and Susie's in France
which has no relevance to anything and I haven't got a cheese sandwich and
somewhere there must be meaning but in the meantime I'd like to have a cold,
just a short one, please, so I can feel justified in moaning

and beyond that
            there is everything

turning like a telescope at the stars.

Dusty

The dust lay all about, from the birth
of the cosmos my physicist said,
and I lay prone, in exhaustion,
or was it surrender I wondered?

I inspected some particles: fine
was their form and attraction
tingled on their surface. Carbon,
I thought, is what animates

I like you I like, and darker too,
dislike. A sigh's breath came
from me and some dust rose
as if into life, like an answer

to a sneeze. Comets plunged
through my head and I saw it:

dust, particles, love, life, all.

Hotelier HD

Depigmenter Russell Square tinct, remote hire attic
creeks, thin lips blooms buried. Archaea achaea, link
skates, johnnie-me-buoy, condom minimum own us,
lynx tyger elias, ashmole hey no nonny john smith,
william bleaks hus, liber camden luds correspondent sos
high hit I caughts, linux povray trace.

Persistence of vision, Haralds werod shouts '*Ut ut ut*'.
On Stamford terrace or cross Saint Andrews Bridge.
Gainstay norm fought, year romany hera ward, nat
Roman he hath. *Aquae Sulis*.

Same day grey wear orb urb us, those business mean
soots. Agen room on rheum, agen morgen bryht, by
skivvies slaved, lay'd mourning, financial pinks toe line
underfoot wh'err era love us onlie shd.

Terence

you were nine months old
and cute in your photographs
and the doctor
(who was an eduma-cated man)
refused your parents
a bed for you.

There was nothing wrong
he told your brickie dad
just a baby's
little cough. (As in smoke-stack

land, as in pea-souper world, as in
good soldiers, like your father, name and number,
always obeyed officers.)

This was 1952 and just before
that terrible day
when they dared defy
that important man

(your mother was a cleaner
with shaky hands, having lost
a thumb on a guillotine press)

and took you up
to the big bare and brick
edifice of cures and death.

It was pneumonia

they said, and you died
within a day.

I grew up

with your ghost on my shoulder

as if you were writing me.

Indjebana-man

Indjebana swam before the black foot trod,
knowing blood-fear, smaller than that Mana-being,
that tooth-gated mouth, that tiger-shark. But blue,
but twisting Indjebana bodies flung at the sun,
playing salt-water waves. Dinginjabana-man led
their pod, loud-talk-maker, bold-fluke-bearer.

Ganadja, she swam with that man, but deepdived
down to the sea-bed builders, those bailer-shell,
Yakuna called by their wisdom-name. Yakuna
that all things knew. Their Baringgwa-word, with that
she dreamtalked, subtler than sea-turn and hum.

In Dinginjabana anger swam, but twisting, but blue
flexing taut tail muscle, thrashing at the green
gulf-water sound. Downworlds, he hurled, overturned
Yakuna spilling onto deep-founder-sands, wise
Yakuna helpless as spawn. Then Baringgwa evil-named
the dolphin-man: "own-sound self-singer, troubler
of reefed coral order, mouth that speaks but noise."

Ganadja knew. She begged her dolphin-man. But blue,
but twisting he moved unmoved by woman pleas.
Ganadja knew. She sank back down to those bailer-shell:
like a tired god of an outworn mode, old
Baringgwa waited at the end of all it knew,
dreamtold Ganadja of a time-beginning crime,
how the jealous with which she swam, Dinginjabana-man,
held no hold on the blood-surge his being held. Blood
that would swim through the world as Yakuna died.
As the Mana swam. "Look", it cried, "on my fluted shell."

She saw into fissured patterns, tectonic tattoos
beaten on its shell. She saw her Dinginjabana dead,
halved an equation into equal parts. She saw
her Indjebana kind, torn flesh in machined lines
of Mana teeth. She saw her own life saved,
hidden under sea-bed sand by Baringgwa-word.
Baringgwa who began to end. Who called the Mana-tribe.

Then Indjebana-spirit dried. Then blackfoot began,
walking without memory on the sun-watched plains.
Then through Ganadja the silver dolphins grew,
sized stronger than that Mana being. Man-Dinginjabana
began to know, watching from the beach that blue,
that twisting limbless struggled, stranded, died.
Ganadja his bride. And the voice within, alive.

Eros, Thanatos, Psyche

The lawn gathered itself together and love
descended to my surprised eyes from wide
opened unexpected skies. Delicate, fine-boned,
the creature was and an odour of like
drizzled through the air in moist tender
similes. And then something stung. But a god
it is, I exclaimed, as pain barbed into my
wounded arm. Harm, I protested, and
the deity rotted while tears stung my eyes.
It stank at me. Morgue exuded from its pores.
You were love, I complained, as stench
gathered on the surfaces of disgust.

I told those skies, this is wrong, and all
of nothing answered with no, no and no.
Love, I cried, and a fluttering began,
as if the air held my hand, and something

other than before came down, holding
in cupped hands, an emptiness that meant
all. And the fullness of that void

shaped form, and lostness trembled
as the air reformed its chords.
It was nothing it was more than enough.

How bad the smell

lurks in the armpits, the groin, the mouth

with the persistence of a body rotting. Recommended it is, I speak in
reversals, to use a preventive hygiene, you know, the scour and scrub kind,
like an air-strike on microbes. But pollution holds, almost imperial in
presence. It has a flavour of war.

I shall protest. I shall never again clean my toilet. I shall abscond from
the notion of baths. I want to stink like the world and roll in metaphors
like faeces. I want to talk about the dirt

      that our planet
                  gives life from

and never be born like this again.

Janus

A sudden cerulean trilby
landed on my head

telling of a broad plain
like summer. Remember?

Antecedent (so the blue
constable said)

to the shadows I unwrapped
believing myself meant

to like them. As if kittens.
But the shadows they talk ribbons

through the long Glamis
nights of Macbeth.

Lollocks

Pliant the particles and pleats of speech were, and resting verbs
lollocked in the sun. 'Lollocked?' a Yellow-beaked bird
enquired with askance from the desk. 'Quite so' the Author
magnanimously replied, as he tickled his quill. His feathered
friend peered (the quill was no relation) and pondered
on quiz, on diction and the airy. The sun withdrew
and the verbs shivered. 'No more lollocking today'
one cried and they ganged back to their wording places.
In trenches, entrenched, armies of definitions
stared across plains. A huge shadow, like the wings
of a giant bird, cast over them and inside,
which was also outside, the Author feathered
his thoughts on a waiting magnum of next.

The Animal Subsides

The animal subsides, like a slow breath,
the animal dies. And all falls away
into the inevitable waiting rhyme
of death. The delayed chime,
so obvious, the bell calls
'oblivion', as memories detach
like seeds. Ring-a-ling-ding.
('s baby talk) Seeds of dandelion.
I have a cupful of smoke in my hands.
I have a cloud drifting in my head.